God in the Winter

13 Devotions and Bible Studies for Women

Valeece Simmons-Davis

VSD

Printed in the United States of America

This book is dedicated to my Vessa, my mother, who left a legacy of faith, hope, and love.

"There is a time for everything, and a season for every activity under the heavens..."

ECCLESIASTES 3:1 NIV

Contents

About the Author

The last thing I wish to do is bore you with credentials that qualify me for such a book. Instead, I'd rather take you on a brief, spiritual journey in which none of my formal education qualifies me. I'll point you in the direction of and credit the education of the Holy Spirit, God's spirit that simply guided me. As I navigated some of life's valleys and mountain peaks, God gave me a vision for studying the Bible spiritually, not routinely or religiously. However, he gave me a longing to study simply because of who he is.

I grew up in a small town, DeRidder, Louisiana. My parents taught me about faith. They taught me about loving God, trusting him, and abiding in his word. Throughout my life, this is what I believed I had done. At least, this was the case until my mother passed away in 2020. I was 32 years old. When she passed, I seriously did not like it, and I told God how angry I was about it. As a child throwing a tantrum over not having his or her way, I threw an adult-like tantrum because God took my mother before I thought it was time. There was so much we planned to do. My father said, "God makes no mistake." One of my dear aunts told me, "See beyond the grave." One of my sweet cousins told me, "No matter what, God still loves you." When my God-brother, who is also my cousin, presented the sermon at my mother's funeral, he said, "She was Lord's to give and Lord's to take away." When he said this, I don't remember if I hollered or began to weep louder. However, I do remember this: I felt like I had died inside. My physical body was still functioning, and my heart still pumped blood. My spirit, however, felt totally crushed. To make a long story short, I was completely heartbroken. No one could comfort me. I suffered a year of deep depression and dreaded each holiday. My first Mother's Day without my mother was the worst! Upon the anniversary of her passing, I began to have hope again, but God was still working on me.

In 2022, things took a huge turn for the better. I had a spark in me that wanted to take courses about ministry and be more involved with God's work. Therefore, I took four courses and enriched myself with history of the Bible, hermeneutics, spirit-filled churches, and having a focused ministry. At the time, the leader of our woman's ministry encouraged me to register for a training. The purpose of the training was to assist her with facilitating our women's Bible studies. While I had dabbed in teaching Bible study or Sunday school in previous years, this experience showed me that their are higher expectations and care that should be taken with God's word. I took the course, and it was one of the best decisions I made. It empowered me to study God strategically, and I have been blessed in ways I could not fathom ever since. I gained more confidence in studying the Holy Bible, and studying in this manner took me to a higher level in God. It took my pain and worry away. It replaced it with unspeakable, unshakeable peace.

Often, I will read God's word for pleasure and self-reflection. This is mainly because I want to relax in a quiet atmosphere and enjoy the word. However, weekly, I study line by line on purpose. When I study line by line with utmost intentions, the Holy Spirit provides more wisdom and understanding. The Holy Spirit is my teacher, and the Holy Bible is my curriculum. God's word armors me, helps me checkmate demons, and allows me to walk in the joy and blessings awaiting me. However, the overflow of blessings and joy I feel would not have happened if I had not taken a step to study spiritually, not routinely.

I pray this way of studying blesses other women and their daughters the way it has blessed me. When one woman is blessed, her whole circle is blessed. God's word simply catches fire!

Introduction

Each Bible study is outlined strategically for you to have a consistent habit of weekly study. May you realize God wants you to live a purpose-driven life through the study of his word. The more time you spend with God, the more your eyes will open to things previously hidden. What rejoicing is in store for you! Praise him in advance, my sister. God is doing a new thing! You will love every bit of it.

Reflect upon the preparation for each week, which is outlined below. Press into the moment of your time set aside for God with intentionality. Each week you are basically having about an hour or two of church all to yourself, just you and God. Ask another spiritual sister to join you with this study and learn together! Get your Bible ready, your aroma therapy going, a warm beverage, your favorite blanket, and anticipate the goodness of God that awaits you.

Weekly Outline

Title for the Week – Reflects main thought.

Key Question – A guiding question for you to apply what God's word requires of you.

Opening Prayer – A way to always lean into God's word before studying to check your heart posture, allowing the presence of the Holy Spirit to teach you as you study.

Devotion – A short, relatable message to set the tone for your Bible study.

Key Verse – The verse you may want to remember, jot for future reference, and share with someone else.

Bible Study – Scripture readings, cross-references, and guiding questions will assist you with conceptual learning of the word. You will learn the word line by line. We cannot lean into the truth of life without reflecting on the word of God. A study Bible is highly recommended and would be great to use. These Bibles typically have cross-references and commentaries. However, you can use credible online resources to help you with some of the questions. You will likely want to view maps as visuals in some studies. Maps are usually found in study Bibles, or you can conduct online research. Finally, I suggest a notebook or journal. You will want to write down your takeaways once God reveals all he wants to share in his word. Take as many days as you need! Try to finish before the next week.

Reflect on Key Question – A review of the guiding question posed at the beginning of the Bible study lesson.

Closing Prayer – A way to end the study with reflection because Satan is not happy that you are prioritizing God and committed to the renewing of your mind. Praise God and ask for wisdom as he refines you from the inside out in your daily walk. He will protect you and allow you to live out what you have learned in his word.

Final Tips

Some days you may feel rushed. Some weeks you may not pick up your Bible to study at all. I encourage you not to do either of the aforementioned things. When we rush God's word, we miss out. Do not skip praying, do not skip rereading, and do not skip cross-references. Often, cross-references give you "Ah ha!" moments. It is really incredible! Set your atmosphere and time aside. Plan time in your calendar like you plan everything else! Plan approximately 2 hours per week. Split this time over days or schedule one day. No matter what you decide, study on purpose! God always comes first! If we make time for everything else, except loving on God and his word, what does this say about us and our priorities? Hey, I've been there. I knew better. Now, I do better.

Welcome

Dear Spiritual Sister,

I am elated you are here! Depending on your personality and traditions you love winter, the holiday seasons, and cool weather. On another note, you may love the holidays, but not so much the weather, and long to be engaged in outdoor activities that do not require snow boots, skis, or several layers of clothing to stay warm. No matter your preference, I'm sure you can find joy in this season at this very moment, reflecting on so many things for which to be grateful. When we, as spiritual sisters in Christ, take an act of faith followed by obedience, God sees us. You took an act of faith to have self-guided devotions and Bible studies because you are reading this right now. Furthermore, God sees us in all seasons of life, throughout all seasons of the year.

Now, I do not know all the twisty roads to which life has taken you, but I do know that you are in the land of the living. I know because you are breathing and reading this letter at this moment. May God bless you with 13 weeks of purposeful prayer, devotion, and Bible studies to take you through a lovely winter season.

Your Spiritual Sister in Christ,

Valeece

Week 1: A Touch She Will Never Forget

Key Question

How do I live a life rooted in faith knowing that Jesus Christ is my Savior?

Opening Prayer

Father God, thank you for sending your son Jesus to walk upon the earth. I declare that Jesus is my Lord and Savior who paid the guarantee when he died on the cross for my sins. Lord, as I begin to study your word, help me see clearly. Help me see how to refine my Christian walk to reflect the message that Jesus is indeed my Lord and Savior, my healer. Give me a clean heart with a heart posture towards you. Remove the scales from my eyes and clarify how I need to use my life to build your kingdom. In Jesus' name, Amen!

Devotion

Are you part of the Christmas rush?! Presents here, online shopping there, decorations everywhere. I am always game for Christmas because of the food, treats, and surprise visits from friends or family members who I have not seen in a very long time! Before you know it, Christmas will have come and gone. In previous years, I wondered if I truly had the time to enjoy Christmas. Such a beautiful time of year seemed so short, and when my mother passed away, I dreaded the holidays. It seemed too difficult to be joyful and smile with a broken heart. To this day, I miss her cooking, her laugh, and our daily chats about anything and everything. However, I thank God for a healed heart. I was saved from an abyss of anger and frustration placed upon a foundation of pain. When I started to seek God's word, he unveiled the beauty in death. The beauty of dying in Christ. When I accepted his will for my life and sought his word, I surrendered the pain to God. From that moment on, I have felt free.

Jesus was the word in the beginning who became flesh to free us from a spiritual death caused by a life of sin. In my opinion, Christmas doesn't get any better than this! What has God healed you from lately? Is there anything you need to surrender so you can be free?

Key Verse

"He said to her, 'Daughter, your faith has healed you. Go in peace and be freed from your suffering.'"

Mark 5:34 NIV

Bible Study

Read Mark 5:21 – 34.

Who wrote the book of Mark?

Who is the author's original audience?

When was this book written?

Look at Verses 21 – 24.

Where is the setting? What happened in verse 21?

Look up the cross-references. What do you learn about the area near the lake? Was this a familiar place to find Jesus?

Mark 4:1
Matthew 9:1

What did the synagogue leader do in verse 22? What was

his name?

Look up the cross-references concerning synagogue leaders. Was Jairus your typical synagogue leader? Were synagogue leaders under pressure from others in the synagogues for following Jesus?

Luke 13:14-16
Acts 13:15
Acts 18:8, 17

What did the synagogue leader ask Jesus to do in verse 23? Describe his issue?

Look up the cross-references. What else do you learn about Jesus when he "lays hands" on someone?

Matthew 19:13-15
Mark 6:5; 7:32; 8:23, 16:18
Luke 4:40; 13:13
Acts 6:6

How did Jesus respond to the synagogue leader in verse 24? Why do you believe a crowd was following and pressing around Jesus in verse 24? Let the Holy Spirit guide you.

Look at verses 25 – 30.

Who was there in verse 25? What was this person's condition?

What else do you learn about how someone with the woman's condition was viewed?

Review Leviticus 15:25 – 30.

How long did she have this condition? Was the woman desperate? Why?

What did the woman do? What obstacle was in her way? Note verse 27.

What did the woman think? Note the quote in verse 28.

What happened in verse 29 and 30? What does this say about Jesus? How do you believe the woman felt?

Look at verses 31 – 34.

How did the disciples respond to Jesus' question? Why did they respond this way in verse 31? What did Jesus do in verse 32? What did the woman who was healed do next in verse 33?

How did Jesus respond to her in verse 34? What can be said about the woman and her belief?

Have you ever been so desperate for healing that you chased for Jesus through a crowd (or whatever your obstacle may have been) to get a touch from the Lord? Have you ever suffered for years? How did it feel when you were freed?

Have you ever felt immediate healing due to having the faith of this woman in the passage? If you have not experienced what the woman in this passage experienced, or if you need healing right now, how can you experience it? What burden do you need to lay at Jesus' feet to get your "touch" from the Lord. If desired, take time to write these thoughts in a journal.

If you haven't already done so, take time to read Biblical commentaries or other cross-references, as needed, to help you consolidate what you learned.

Review Key Question

How do I live a life rooted in faith knowing that Jesus Christ is my Savior?

Closing Prayer

Father God, you have been so good. Thank you for reminding me that my Savior lives! I can come to Jesus with any problem, and he will free me of it. As he healed the woman with the issue of blood, I can be healed by my faith, too. One touch from you will change me for a lifetime! Thank you for reminding me how to show my faith by my behavior. During this Christmas season, I will center all my focus upon this fact: My savior lives! Jesus, I praise you for healing me and making me whole. Because of you, Jesus, I lack nothing. I have everything I need. In Jesus' name, Amen!

Week 2: No Fear, Just Belief

Key Question

How can I overcome fear amid a terrible ordeal? How can I use this as my testimony to others?

Opening Prayer

Gracious Lord, thank you for not giving me a spirit of fear, but of power, love, and a sound mind. I know you are a healer. I need you to rid me of unbelief and fear so I can have all that you have in store for me. I want and need your help now more than ever. Help me to not be afraid. Reveal your desires in this study. I want to receive all you have for me. In Jesus' name, Amen!

Devotion

When the new year approaches, I always try to do several things. Firstly, I make sure we have a good menu. Traditionally, we cook pork chops, black-eyed peas, rice, and cabbage. This is the dinner we cook because, as a child, I was told it brings blessings in the new year. At least, this is what has been shared with me over the years concerning this menu. Even though I never associated this dinner with blessings throughout the year, I enjoy eating it anyway! Who does not like a good homecooked, southern meal?

Next, in previous years, I stayed up until midnight to pray into the new year. Sometimes, I would attend what my family calls "Watch Night," a church service that ends by praying into the new year. My mother and I would go to this service, and it would end with a beautiful, heartfelt prayer to kick-start the new year. It was just what we needed to step into a new season! Now, however, I just make sure I say a prayer before I fall asleep. Staying out late is not really my thing in this "season" of my life. Pun intended.

One way I have leveled up my focus on God in the new year was by adding a period of fasting. My husband, children, and I fast as a family now. When we did this for the first time, as a family, not just a routine, God revealed some things to me about my husband, my children, and me I had not previously noticed. These changes were subtle, yet impactful. For example, we were much more focused on positivity, yearned for complete joy and happiness, and didn't stay in ruts long. I believe this was made known because this time our family fasted and prayed together: touching, agreeing, and believing in unity.

As the year progressed, God clarified more things about how to refine my Christian walk. When I tell you I was stretched, I was STRECHED! Although this stretching felt like terrible mid-life growing pains, I had healing. I had restoration I had not felt in years passed. Even my children began to flourish in a different way, becoming more patient and intuitive. Their faith became more evident, and the light of Jesus in them began to shine even brighter for others to see. How do my husband and I know? People who interacted with our children, such as their teachers or church staff, shared things about them with us. Sometimes, our kids have spoken with Godly wisdom out of nowhere, and we, as parents, would be so proud at the work God was doing in them.

I realized there are higher levels to which God is calling me. He is calling my circle of family and friends to higher levels as well. In the beginning, I was excited about all this overflow. As some unprecedented trials started to appear, I became afraid. When I went to God in prayer and read his word in the book of James, I realized these trials were a testing of my faith. Therefore, I believed. I still believe.

If a person does not believe his or her prayers or believe God will follow through on his promises, it is written in the book of James that this person should not expect to receive anything from the Lord. Now, I see the fruits of my belief, and I see what I was missing due to fear. I thank God for wisdom that changed my perspective through the study of his word. I am not the same because of it. I also have more joy because of it!

Key Verse

"Don't be afraid; just believe."

Mark 5:36 NIV

Bible Study

Reread Mark 5:21 – 34.

Read Mark 5:35 – 43.

Who wrote the book of Mark?

Who is the author's original audience?

When was this book written?

Look at verses 21 – 34.

Recall what happened in these verses.

Recall the synagogue leader? What did he do?

Why was a crowd following Jesus?

What happened to the woman with the blood condition? How was her issue resolved?

Look at verses 35 – 40.

What did people tell the synagogue leader about his daughter in verse 35?

What did Jesus tell Jairus in verse 36?

Who followed Jesus to Jairus' home in verse 37?

What were people doing in verse 38?

What did Jesus say in verse 39?

How did the people respond in verse 40? Why do you believe the people responded this way. Ask the Holy Spirit to guide you.

What did Jesus do in verse 40? Who was left with Jesus in the house?

Look at verses 41-43.

What did Jesus do in verse 41? What did he say and to whom does he say it? What does "*Talitha koum!*" mean in English?

What happened in verse 42? How old was the little girl? How did people respond?

What were Jesus' orders in verse 43? Why did Jesus say this? Look at the cross-reference Matthew 8:4. What do you learn about why Jesus said what he said in verse 43?

If you haven't already done so, take time to read Biblical commentaries or other cross-references, as needed, to help you consolidate what you learned.

Review Key Question

How can I overcome fear amid a terrible ordeal? Why is believing so important?

Closing Prayer

Gracious Lord, thank you for performing miracles so that I may believe and have an encounter with you. Give me a heart not to run after you for simply what you can do for me or what I can see you do for someone else, but God, remind me that I should chase you just because of who you are! The same healing people experienced during Biblical times is the same healing I can have right now. I trust you. As soon as I close my Bible study, something may present itself to steal the joy I have found in this time with you. Lord, please allow me to remain in your presence all week long. Refresh my spirit every day to walk in belief and favor. In Jesus' name, Amen!

Week 3: Not Built to Give Up

Key Question

Have you ever been persistent with chasing God to ensure you get justice or the provision you need? How has God shown you that he freely gives because he is just that good?

Opening Prayer

Heavenly Father, as a woman of Christ, I know things may get tough for me at times. However, you did not create me to give up. You created me to be persistent with things that are aligned in your will, not my own. Your word teaches patience and trust in you. If I have been wronged, you are a God of justice. If I am in need, you are a provider, God. I can come to you persistently with all my cares and concerns. You know what I need before I ask. Still, you want me to pursue you, and that's just what I will do. Help me with my pursuit. In Jesus' name, Amen!

Devotion

Are you guilty of a New Year's resolution? What is that anyway? By the time people have entered week 4 or week 5 of the new year, most people are no longer upholding those things they promised themselves or others. Why do you think the title of week 3 is "Not Built to Give Up"? I want you to remain committed to the good things God placed in your heart. Remain steady with promises you made to yourself or your family. Ask God to sustain you so that you will reach the next level in him. There is so much joy there...so much joy.

I have made resolutions of my own. However, I have also dealt with the consequences of not keeping such resolutions, which included not stepping up when God had called me to do so. When God called me out of darkness and pain from the loss of my mother, and I obeyed his call, I had so much joy. I felt brand new. I thought I knew what joy was, but God showed me more. He showed me how dependent I was on my way of doing things.

Unknowingly, I focused more on my grief, sorrow, and self-pity above God's blessings. I was angry about the loss of my mother, my Vessa. When I was not operating at my best, my husband picked up the slack. Marriage is not always 50/50. In my case, it was Valeece, zero, and Jarome, 100, for quite some time. I am not ashamed to say it. In fact, I will say it because it is my testimony. It shows the mighty long way from which God brought me!

From then on, I made a resolution, not at the beginning of the year, but in June of 2022 that I would never let myself get back to that dark place. I feel too good where I am now! Why even think about looking back? With that said, what resolution do you need to make and stick to with the help of God? May you be encouraged to take the first step. Now, let's get into this Bible study.

Key Verse

"However, when the Son of Man comes, will he find faith on the earth?"

Luke 18:8 NIV

Bible Study

Read Luke 18: 1 – 8.

Who wrote the book of Luke?

Who is the author's original audience?

When was this book written?

Look at verses 1 – 3.

What type of reading is this?

What is a parable? Who is telling this parable?

Who is listening to the parable?

Why is the parable being shared?

Who are the main persons in this parable?

What is the woman's request?

Look at verses 4 – 5.

What can you say about the judge's character? What kind of man is he?

Did the woman receive justice from the judge?

Why did the judge make his decision to help the woman?

Look at the cross-references. What else do you learn about persistence, waiting, and praying?

Isaiah 40:31
Luke 11:5-11
Acts 1:14
Romans 12:12
Ephesians 6:18
Colossians 4:2
1 Thessalonians 5:16-17

Look at verses 6 – 8.

What did Jesus say in verses 6-7? What point did Jesus emphasize concerning the unjust judge's decision to help the woman versus his desire to help us as a gracious God?

Look at these cross-references. What else do you learn about how God cares for his people?

Luke 7:11-17
Exodus 22:22-23

How does Jesus end this reading in verse 8? Why is his question so important here? What is he telling us we need to do concerning our faith? (Go back to verse 1.)

Look at these cross-references. What else do you learn about people's faith and the cost to follow Jesus? Do we all take Jesus as seriously as we should?

Matthew 8:18-22
Matthew 16:24-27

Are you persistent with praying and never giving up as it is written in God's word? If not, how will you change? Do you know the cost of following Jesus?

If you haven't already done so, take time to read Biblical commentaries or other cross-references, as needed, to help you consolidate what you learned.

Review Key Question

Have you ever been persistent with chasing God to ensure you get justice or the provision you need? How has God shown you that he freely gives because he is just that good?

Closing Prayer

Heavenly Father, you are good. Thank you for sending Jesus to teach us in parables, in ways we can understand and apply even now. Lord, I will commit to praying. I will be persistent with coming to you with my problems instead of the world. If an unjust judge will give a women justice after being bothered time and time again, how much more would my good, good father in heaven give me everything I need and more?! Thank you for teaching me your word. Keep me close, now and forever. In Jesus' name, Amen!

Week 4: Remember Me

Key Question

When in anguish, how can you use prayer, asking God to remember you and to deliver you from such hurt?

Opening Prayer

Lord Almighty, you are the sovereign God, and you reign supreme. I know who you are. I, your servant, am here again. Remember me? I am the one you formed in my mother's womb, knitting me to be in your likeness. I know talking to you can do so much for me. Whether in a place of misery or a place of joy, you hear all the words that flow from my mouth. Thank you, Lord, in advance for remembering me and hearing all my requests. You never grow tired of me. Despite my faults, you still provide. Once I pray, remind me to listen to you and act on what the Holy Spirit tells me. Lord, I do not want to move before you say move. Give me wisdom. Press your word upon my heart for this study. May the Holy Spirit be present. In Jesus' name, Amen!

Devotion

Wow! We are in week four of the winter season. Christmas décor is usually taken down by now. Some people take a little longer than others to remove decorations. Nevertheless, to each his own. Some people keep Christmas trees up year-round and change the decoration to match the current season. One thing that should remain, whether your Christmas decorations do or not, is your prayer life. Remember, you may get weary, but doing what

God tells you to do is righteous in his sight. You must talk to God and listen to him in prayer. This is a fundamental Christian responsibility. Whatever you must do to have a fervent, consistent prayer life, do it!

Praying more deliberately and praying more often has blessed my soul. In my younger days, I mainly prayed when things were bad. Now, however, I really pray in all seasons!

Anyone who grew up in a traditional southern Baptist church knows that prayer occurs before and after just about everything. I do mean EVERYTHING! I'm sure this is customary in other churches as well. When I was little, I used to think, "Are we really praying again?" It tickled me. I would even make jokes about how certain people prayed. I would know how long certain people in the church were going to pray due to their patterns. I knew if "Brother A" prayed, the prayer may be 5 minutes, but if "Brother B" prayed, we may be here 10 minutes. I usually made these predictions during alter call. I may have even acted out a few of those prayers for fun with my friends.

Let's shift gears. Now that I am old, guess who does not laugh about praying anymore? In fact, guess who is praying over anything and everything now. Me! I have seen how God works when I pray intentionally. The more I pray and act in obedience, the more I am inclined to hear God because I formed a habit of hearing God. I am more patient because he unveils blessings I would not have received if I had not listened to the Holy Spirit. Here is a true story: I prayed to have a son as my firstborn, and I have him. Here is another true story: I prayed for a daughter as my second born, and I have her. In fact, I got her and the little attitude that goes with it. That is a different story and a different Bible study for another day!

Remember this: Even if you do not get exactly what you prayed, God has a divine plan for your life. He may be saying, "Not yet," "Not at all," or "Not in the way you think it will be." However, he is sovereign, and he knows what is best for you. Trust His will for your life, not your own. When I act before God says I should act, I am quickly reminded to pray and wait. Why? Because things do not work out well. The good news is that the cycles of impatience reduce because I have formed a habit of prayer and waiting. Therefore, I receive more blessings.

Listen, my Spiritual Sister, there are so many distractions. Life, kids, husbands, family, friends, work, other peoples' problems, social media, and the list goes on. However, you must prioritize your prayer life and act on your prayer life. If you do not have a prayer life, you need to get one. Get it fast because you are missing out, my Spiritual Sister.

Key Verse

"So in the course of time, Hannah became pregnant and gave birth to a son. She named him Samuel saying, "Because I asked the Lord for him."

1 Samuel 1:20 NIV

Bible Study

Read 1 Samuel 1:1 – 20.

Who wrote the book of 1 Samuel?

Who is the author's original audience?

When was the book written?

Look at verses 1 – 8.

How does this story begin? Who is Elkanah?

Where was Elkanah from?

How many wives did Elkanah have? What were their names? What was the difference between Elkanah's wives?

In verse 3, where did Elkanah go year after year?

What else do you learn about Elkanah's travel to Shiloh year after year from the cross-references? Why was this travel important?

Joshua 18:1

Deuteronomy 12:5-7

Exodus 23:14-17

Exodus 34:22-23

Luke 2:41

How did Elkanah give portions to both his wives? Why?

Who was Hannah's rival? What did she do? What does this say about the rival's character?

How did the rival make Hannah feel year after year? Did Hannah's husband address her needs?

Look at verses 9 – 18.

What did Hannah do after they finished eating? Who was sitting on a chair near the doorpost of the Lord's house in verse 9?

What did Hannah do in verse 10? Look at the cross-references to gain more insight about how Hannah prayed and her belief. What do you learn about God remembering his people?

Genesis 8:1; 28:20; 29:32

Judges 13: 1-5

As Hannah kept praying, what did Eli notice in verse 13?

What did Eli believe was Hannah's issue? What did he say?

How did Hannah clarify what was wrong to Eli? How was she feeling in verses 15-16?

How did Eli respond to Hannah after she explained? What else do you learn from these cross-references about "go in peace" and God's character.

Judges 18:6
1 Samuel 25:35
Genesis 30:22
Mark 5:34
Psalms 20:3-5

How did Hannah respond to Eli in verse 18? Why do you think her face changed? Did Eli's words bless her? Look at these cross-references to gain more insight.

Ruth 2:13
Ecclesiastes 9:7
Romans 15:13

Look at verses 19-20.

What happened in verse 19? Who went back home at Ramah?

What happened later in verse 19 between Elkanah & Hannah? Did God remember Hannah's prayer from verse 11?

What happened to Hannah in verse 20? What was the gender of her baby?

What did Hannah name her baby? Why?

What did Hannah's experience teach you about the Lord?

If you haven't already done so, take time to read Biblical commentaries or other cross-references, as needed, to help you consolidate what you learned.

Review Key Question

When in anguish, how can you use prayer, asking God to remember you and to deliver you from such hurt?

Closing Prayer

Lord Almighty, there is no doubt you showed up for Hannah in her time of need. You are consistent in your ways. I know you will show up for me just as you showed up for Hannah! Hannah left in peace because she knew you deliver on all your promises! She knew you would remember her. You saw how she was treated by her rival, Penninah, and you felt her pain. I know if I pray and seek you with a sincere heart, you will hear me and remember me. May your will be done in me. In Jesus' name. Amen!

Week 5: Committed

Key Question

How can I remain obedient after God blesses me with what I requested from him?

Opening Prayer

Daddy God, thank you for hearing all my prayers. Even when I may not know what to say or how to say it, the Holy Spirit intercedes for me. You shape up my heart and align it to your desires so that I may live in your fullness. As I study your word and learn more about Hannah's willingness to follow through on her commitment to you, I ask that you help me do the same. In Jesus' name, Amen!

Devotion

I live in the southern states where there is not much snow. When I was a little girl, I would see snow on television in cartoons or movies, not on an iPad or cell phone. Smart devices did not exist at that time! Anyway, I thought it would be so cool if it snowed. Finally, one day, it did snow! I could not believe it. It was beautiful and winter white. I marveled at the idea that it snowed in Southwest Louisiana. I cherished the snow by walking in it, touching it, forming a snowball, and whatever else I could do until it melted completely around mid-day.

Think of a time when your parents, grandparents, or parental figure granted you a request when you really wanted something. Perhaps, it was a toy, a car on your 16th birthday, or a special outing. You may have mentioned or agreed to certain behavioral expectations upon receiving this request. How did you feel once you received this blessing from your parents? Did you remain obedient to what you said you would do?

Often, we receive blessings from the Lord but forget to follow through as servants to him. We make promises, and sometimes, we do not uphold them. A fleshly, sinful nature is the cause. This is no secret. However, when you are truly a servant of the Lord and acknowledge him as your master, you do not have the desire to want your desires anymore. You only want what God wants. Remember, we want fewer cycles of doing things our way. If there is a true change in us, it is evident in our behavior. No matter the cost to us, we say, "Your will be done, Lord."

Key Verses

"I prayed for this child, and the Lord has granted me what I asked of him. So now, I give him to the Lord. For his whole life he will be given over to the Lord.' And he worshiped the Lord there."

1 Samuel 1:27-28 NIV

Bible Study

Reread 1 Samuel 1:1-20.

Read 1 Samuel 1:21-28.

Read 1 Samuel 2:1-10.

Who wrote the book of 1 Samuel?

Who is the author's original audience?

When was the book written?

Look at 1 Samuel 1:21-23.

After Hannah had her baby, where was her husband going in verse 21? What else do you learn in Deuteronomy 12:11?

What did Hannah say to her husband in verse 21? How does Hannah's statement connect to Luke 2:22?

How did her husband respond? What else do you learn in Numbers 30:7? Is Hannah obligated to her vow?

Look at 1 Samuel 1:24 – 28.

What did Hannah take her son? What all did she take with her?

After the bull was sacrificed, who did Hannah bring her baby to meet?

What did Hannah say to Eli? Could you have done what Hannah did? Why or why not?

Look at 1 Samuel 2:1-11.

Describe how Hannah's prayer begins. How is she feeling?

What does she say about the Lord in verses 2 and 3?

What else do you learn about the Lord from these cross-references?

Exodus 15:11
Psalm 9:14, 13:5
Psalm 89:17, 24
Deuteronomy 32:30-31

How does Hannah describe the power of God throughout her prayer?

What does Hannah say about wicked people and those who oppose the Lord?

Why was Hannah grateful in her prayer? What did God do for her?

When Elkanah returned home to Ramah in verse 11, what happened to Samuel?

Who trained Samuel? What else do you learn from 1 Samuel 3:1? Who did Samuel become?

What did you learn from Hannah's commitment to God? Is God committed to you?

If you haven't already done so, take time to read Biblical commentaries or other cross-references, as needed, to help you consolidate what you learned.

Reflect on Key Question

How can I remain obedient after God blesses me with what I requested from him?

Closing Prayer

Father God, I call you *Adonai* because you are my master, the Lord over my life. Thank you for all you have taught me in this Bible study. You show your concern for me even when I am hurting, turning my sadness into joy. I praise you for who you are. You are a healer who takes the shame and pain away. I am your daughter. You look after me. If I seek you first as a child seeking the help of a parent, Daddy God, I know all things will be added to me according to your will for my life. I praise you with my prayers and acknowledge the things you do in my life. I will share my testimony so others will know the great works you have done. In Jesus' name, Amen!

Week 6: Eternal Life

Key Question

Why did God send his son, and what does this mean to me?

Opening Prayer

Lord Jesus, I pray the word of God manifests who you are to me plainly and clearly. I know who you are but help me know that I truly know who you are! Root it so far down in my soul that none of Satan's schemes work against the peace, love, and joy I have found in you. No man can take away what you have given me. Let my belief be so strong that it is contagious. In Jesus' name, Amen!

Devotion

Love is powerful. In fact, love can make you do some crazy, irrational things if you allow it. It will make you spend lots of money on people you adore. It will encourage you to give up everything and place your own wants or needs above someone else's wants or needs. It will make you buy up the store on Valentine's Day.

Love will turn a kind, mild-mannered woman into a savage momma bear when it comes to her children. Love will turn a quiet, loving father into a fighting beast when it comes to his children. If you think you won't do anything totally dramatic when you have children, have some and find out! I will admit, before I had children, my attitude was different, way different. I was quiet and let a lot of things go. I was pretty passive. To an extent, if I felt wronged, I would try to shrug things off and tolerate it. When my son came into the picture, all that changed. In fact, God had to tell me to calm down! I could hear a little voice say, "Okay, Valeece. You are doing a little too much."

Now, when it comes to my husband, things get even crazier. If you really know me, you KNOW how I am about my husband. I will fight a mob over him knowing I will lose, but believe me, I will go out swinging! I love my husband, and there is a song that says, "In my world, only you, can make me do for love what I would not do." Help me, Lord! God is still working on me.

Let's take a look at Jesus. He looks at us the same way we look at our loved ones today. God loves his children. He makes sure our needs are met. Why you ask? Because of love. God loved us first! As imperfect as we are, look at what we will do as an act of love for our spouses, children, friends, and family. For those we love, we would try to remove any barrier in the way to show them we care. There are no barriers between us and God except sin. But guess what? Jesus removed the burden of sin a long time ago on the cross. He paid our debt. A debt we could not and would not pay. You, beloved, have the choice to repent and accept Christ as your savior. He loves you. Will you show God that you love him, too?

Key Verse

"For God so loved the world that he gave his one and only son, that whoever believes in him shall not perish but have eternal life."

John 3:16 NIV

Bible Study

Read John 3:1-21.

Who wrote the book of John?

Who was the author's original audience?

When was the book written?

Look at verses 1-9.

How is Nicodemus described in verse 1? What else do you learn about him in John 7:50-51?

What did Nicodemus say when he went to Jesus in verse 2? What do you learn from Acts 2:22-24 and Acts 10:38 that connects to verse 2?

How did Jesus respond in verse 3? What was the question Nicodemus asked next? Did he understand what Jesus meant by being "born again"?

What did Jesus say next to help the pharisee understand? What else do you learn about being "born again" in Titus 3:5?

What did Nicodemus ask next in verse 9?

Look at verses 10-15.

What does Jesus say in verse 10-15? Read these cross-references for more insight about what Jesus is teaching Nicodemus. What does it teach you?

Luke 2:46
John 1:18; 6:38; 7:16-17; 8:28; 12:32
Proverbs 30:4
Acts 2:34

Look at verses 16-21.

Why did God send Jesus as flesh to walk among us?

What happens to those who do not believe?

What is said about light and darkness? Why do people love

darkness instead of light?

Why do people who hate the light do evil and will not come in the light?

What is said about people who live by the truth?

What else do you learn from the cross-references that connect to the conversation between Jesus and Nicodemus?

Romans 5:8

Ephesians 2:4-5

John 1:4; 5:24 6:29, 40, 57; 8:12; 10:36; 11:42; 12:47; 17:8

1 John 4:9

Ephesians 5:11-13

Why did Jesus come? Did everyone believe back then? Does everyone believe now? Do you believe?

Summarize what you learned about the conversation between Jesus and Nicodemus.

If you haven't already done so, take time to read Biblical commentaries or other cross-references, as needed, to help you consolidate what you learned.

Reflect on Key Question

Why did God send his son, and what does this mean to me?

Closing Prayer

Lord Jesus, you came to save me. You did it because of love. There is no greater love! You died on a cross that was meant for me! This is love I cannot repay and will never repay even if I spent a lifetime trying. I realize that being born again is part of the journey to get into heaven. I must walk in truth to be in the light, not in darkness. I want to share this word with everyone I know. Open the eyes of your children to seek you, repent, and do right in your sight. In Jesus' name, Amen!

Week 7: To Catch a Fox

Key Question

How do couples in courtship and married couples preserve their love under the eyes of God?

Opening Prayer

Lord, I know that marriage was instituted by you with Adam and Eve in the book of Genesis. Marriage will only work if it is led entirely by you. I pray for marriages all over the world. May they align to your will. Lord, if any marriages are broken, please fix the heart postures of both spouses. Satan knows blessed marriages beget blessed children and families for generations to come. Godly marriages can cure generations of sin. Marriages must stay rooted in your word to thrive. In Jesus' name, Amen!

Devotion

Love is in the air! For weeks you have seen Valentine's Day products stocked among all the shelves in the store. This was likely already in the back of the store waiting to come out the day after Christmas. Don't you just love the way stores market these days? Christmas products appear in September, and Valentine's Day products appear right after Christmas. To me, it is quite annoying. Sometimes, however, it reminds me that a new season is coming. Most of the time, however, I am not that far ahead because I am still trying to enjoy the current season. Lord, help!

Spiritual Sister, if you have never experienced a Godly marriage or a Godly relationship that had marriage potential, then I know you will love this study. I know you will love it because God reveals how awesome and wonderful marriage life is when it operates under his authority. Anyone who has had a messy relationship, or an ungodly marriage, will attest to the fact that life can feel absolutely horrible! The selfishness of living in sin rubs off on you, your home has no peace, and the kids cut up because the parents cut up. Help us, Lord!

Here is the good news! God can fix anything! I do not care how tore up your relationship with your spouse may seem. God can fix it if and only if you and your spouse turn with a heart posture towards God. The Devil despises marriage. Why do you think it is so hard to maintain a good one? If it were easy, divorce rates would not be so high. Still, it is not so hard if you and your spouse are rooted in Christ, not self. Divorce is due to sin. Point. Blank. Period.

Be encouraged to share a word with your spouse today or a spiritual sister who needs a positive word about love. If you are not married, but would like to be, think of this study as obtaining wisdom for a future relationship you may have. You never know what is in store for you. Do not count love out! If you want a Godly relationship, ask God for it, but be patient and listen to him.

Key Verse

"Catch for us the foxes, the little foxes that ruin the vineyards, our vineyards that are in bloom."

Song of Songs 2:15 NIV

Bible Study

Read Song of Songs 2:1-17.

Who wrote the Song of Songs?

Who was the initial audience?

When was it written?

Why was it written?

What type of reading is this? A song, poetry, narrative, etc.?

Look at verses 1-7.

In verse 1, how is the woman describing herself? What else do you learn from Isaiah 35:1, 1 Chronicles 27:29, and Song of Solomon 5:13?

In verse 2, how is the man describing his love?

What ceremony is the woman describing in verse 3-7? How do you know? Look at the cross references.

Song of Songs 1:4; 1:14; 3:5, 4:16; 5:8, 7:8; 8:3-4

Esther 1:11

Numbers 1:52

What is her advice or warning to women in verse 7? Why should love and commitment not be rushed on our terms?

Look at verses 8-13.

How does the wife describe her husband in verses 8 and 13? Upon what precious memories is she reflecting? Look at the cross-references for more insight about figs.
Isaiah 28:4
Jeremiah 24:2
Hosea 9:10
Micah 7:1

Look at verses 14-15.

How is the woman described in verse 14?

What is the warning from the husband in verse 15? Why is this important in courtship and in marriage?

Look at verses 16-17.

How does this chapter end?

Are the woman and man in love? How do you know?

If you haven't already done so, take time to read Biblical commentaries or other cross-references, as needed, to help you consolidate what you learned.

Reflect on Key Question

How do couples who are courting and married couples preserve their love under the eyes of God?

Closing Prayer

Lord, thank you for sharing such a poetic word. Obviously, when people are in love with God, they are righteously in love with each other. No one can show love to another person unless he or she loves you more.

May you fix every broken heart due to a divorce. May people be hopeful knowing your love is all they need. You know the needs of everyone, and your will must be done. May they accept your will and heal.

For every marriage, meet the need. If any spouse feels mistreated, abused, neglected, or hurt, may these individuals come to you to surrender their problems, asking for wisdom to guide next steps and peace for the future. For the married couples who are strong in your word, may they maintain unity by drawing upon the power in your word, which has held them together all these years. May they catch the little foxes, and you cancel the assignment of Satan.

Marriage is a beautiful thing when it is orchestrated by you, not by man. In Jesus' name, Amen!

Week 8: See Beyond Me

Key Question

When I do not have an important position as seen by man, how can I act quickly for God's purpose?

Opening Prayer

My Lord, your servant comes to you preparing a heart for another Bible study. Your word teaches us to be selfless. May you increase so that I decrease. For I know if I decrease, the benefits include a closer relationship with you and blessings that I cannot fathom. I put my faith in you. When I am under pressure, and I must act, direct me with the Holy Spirit concerning what I must do. I want to receive all that is in store for me in your word. In Jesus' name, Amen!

Devotion

We are over halfway through winter! The Valentine's Day rush is slowing down. In a few weeks, spring will be knocking on your doorstep. Flowers will bloom, birds will sing, and things will seem to become fruitful and multiply. Pollination will be at full force, and everyone in Louisiana and Texas will have allergy flare ups galore! Get your Zyrtec, Claritin, Benadryl, allergy shots, and everything else to treat allergies lined up!

Turn your attention to the role of a bee. Think about this little bee. A bee goes from one flower to another, spreading pollen from male parts of a flower to female parts of another flower. Many types of flowers rely on this small act from a bee to reproduce. If bees stop being part of the pollination process, many flowers will not reproduce. What a significant impact on a small role of a bee, right?

Well, think about your "small" role in the world God created. What if people having an encounter with God and turning from sin were, in part, dependent upon your obedience and your "small" role in the body of Christ? When a person is saved and turns to God with an act of faith, angels in heaven rejoice! The captive is set free! Those who have been born again are thrilled to have a new member in the body of Christ. Does your role still seem small?

Key Verse

"David said to Abigail, 'Praise be to the Lord, the God of Israel, who has sent you today to me. May you be blessed for your judgement and for keeping me from bloodshed this day and from avenging myself with my own hands.'"

1 Samuel 25:32-33

Bible Study

Read 1 Samuel 25:1-42.

Who wrote the book of 1 Samuel?

Who was the author's original audience?

When was this book written?

Look at verses 1-3.

How does verse 1 begin? Who passed away? What did David do?

Who is mentioned in verse 2? What is true about him? Who was his wife?

Look at verses 4-31.

Why was David in the wilderness? What did he learn about Nabal while he was there? Why was this beneficial news to David?

What were David's instructions to his men? What had David done for Nabal that likely contributed to his wealth?

What did David say and do after he heard Nabal's response? How many men were with David in verse 12?

Was Nabal's response a wise response? Why or why not?

Nabal's wife, Abigail, was informed of the incident between Nabal and David's men in verses 14-17. What did she do next in verse 18? Why did Abigail act so quickly?

What had David said in verse 13 that makes it obvious Abigail was pressed for time? Also, what did David say in verses 20-22?

Summarize what Abigail says to David in verses 23-31. What does she seem to know about David's current situation and his future?

Look at verses 32-42.

Summarize what David said to Abigail in verses 32-35. Why did David praise the Lord for Abigail's quick actions?

David accepted what Abigail brought him and told her to "go in peace." Why is this significant? Was her request granted?

When Abigail returned to her husband, what was he doing

in verse 36? What does this tell you about Nabal's character considering David is the anointed King of Israel?

When did Abigail tell her husband what happened? What happened to Nabal in verses 37-38? Is this surprising to you? How was Nabal described throughout this reading?

When David heard the news about Nabal, why did he praise God in verse 39?

How does the reading end in verses 40-42? What would have happened if Abigail did not act?

If you haven't already done so, take time to read Biblical commentaries or other cross-references, as needed, to help you consolidate what you learned.

Reflect on Key Question

When I do not have an important position as seen by man, how can I act quickly for God's purpose?

Closing Prayer

My Lord, help me see beyond my personal feelings to do your will for a greater cause. Help me be persuasive towards the right people so that harm, whether physical or mental, will not come to others. I see from Abigail's experience that one righteous act had a ripple effect that not only blessed the others involved, but it blessed her, too. I trust your will for my life. I see that if I refrain from acting on my feelings, but only with your wisdom, everything will work out for my good. In Jesus' name, Amen!

Week 9: Woof! Woof!

Key Question

What did Jesus reveal when he encountered the Gentile woman, and how does this apply to me now?

Opening Prayer

Dear Jesus, I am so glad you came to save me. Even though the Jews were your chosen people, your word revealed that your saving grace extended to me, too, a Gentile. You cast out demonic spirits, and because of faith, people can come to you and be healed from sin, sickness, and any disease that tries to come against them. Help me apply the reading that I am about to study. May you teach me and facilitate this lesson. Impress upon my heart what you want me to know about you, Lord. In Jesus' name, Amen!

Devotion

Many people I know are dog owners. I have two dogs myself, Hope and Bear. While Bear is not in favor of rain or wet grounds, she is definitely not a fan of snow. On the contrary, Hope loves the snow! A few years ago, we experienced extreme blizzard-like conditions. Hope enjoyed running outside. She enjoyed slipping and sliding on the snow as it hardened and melted over the yard.

Both Bear and Hope are sweet dogs, and like all dogs, they love it when you share food with them. Particularly, Bear loves to wait patiently near the table while my eight-year-old daughter unintentionally drops small parcels of food on the floor. When Jill is in a good mood, she shares on purpose! Ha!

Isn't it funny how God can reveal his word to you in all the things he has made, including dogs?! For example, Bear did not necessarily want the entire plate of food from which Jill was eating. Bear was content with the crumbs.

Key Verse

"Woman, you have great faith! Your request is granted."

Matthew 15:28 NIV

Bible Study

Read Matthew 15:21-28.

Who wrote the book of Matthew?

Who was the author's original audience?

When was this book written?

Look at verses 21-22.

Where did Jesus go in verse 21? Where was he coming from? See Matthew 15:34-35.

Who was the woman who came to Jesus? Was she a Jew or Gentile? What issue did the woman bring to Jesus?

How did the woman address Jesus? What did she call him?

What else do you learn from the cross references?

Matthew 11:21
Matthew 9:27
Matthew 4:24

Look at verses 23-28.

How did Jesus respond in verse 23? How did the disciples

respond?

What did Jesus say in verse 24?

What else do you learn from these cross references?
Matthew 10:6-23
Romans 15:8

How did the woman respond to Jesus in verse 25? What else do you learn from Matthew 8:2?

What did Jesus say in verse 26?
What did the woman say next in verse 27?
What did Jesus say to the woman in verse 28?

What does the word say happened to her daughter? Did this take a long time or happen instantly?

Take time to read Mark 7:24-30. Did you learn anything else about the Gentile woman and why she sought Jesus?

If you haven't already done so, take time to read Biblical commentaries or other cross-references, as needed, to help you consolidate what you learned.

Reflect on Key Question

What did Jesus reveal when he encountered the Gentile woman, and how does this apply to you now? Did he only come to save Jews, or did he come for Gentiles, too?

Closing Prayer

Dear Jesus, I am totally okay with however you want to bless me. I do not have to have an entire plate of food prepared for me on a table. Lord, if it is your food being served, the crumbs under the table are enough! I'll take the crumbs! Woof! Woof! You blessed the Gentile woman due to her faith. Even though she was not a Jew, you treated her like your own. God, you adopted me. Wow! You never cease to amaze me. Lord, thank you for salvation. In Jesus' name, Amen!

Week 10: Everything I Ever Did?

Key Question

How can you share your encounter with God and reflect your belief in Christ by your testimony?

Opening Prayer

Lord Jesus, there are some things in my life I am not proud to discuss. However, I know I can come to you with anything. I know you are the sacrificial lamb who came to take away the sins of the world. You are coming back again. I am grateful that I recognize who you are so that I may be with you when you return. I praise you for loving me despite my sins. You saved me, and I will never be the same. You graciously give to me, and I am forever thankful. May I testify to others about how you have changed my life. In Jesus' name, Amen!

Devotion

When I was in elementary school, we would make snowflakes by folding a piece of paper in half and cutting out random designs. Of course, no students' snowflakes looked similar. They all had a distinct pattern, uniquely designed by their respective artist.

I used to admire snowflakes and watch snow as it fell. Even as an adult when God would surprise us with snow in the south, I enjoyed watching it from a window. Something about snow was so peaceful and calm. Also, I felt safe knowing I had a warm home to enjoy with my husband and children. This would make perfect weather for my husband to build a fire. The smell of burning wood, the sound of it crackling, the sight of the flames disappearing upward into the chimney, and the warmth I felt as heat radiated to me blessed me. I always laid comfortably on the couch, in my favorite spot with a soft blanket and a warm beverage. This is a feeling of winter I just enjoyed. I still do.

Each of our lives are unique just like snowflakes. Because we serve a sovereign God, he knows everything his children have done throughout their lives. Yes, everything we ever did. Every move we make and every step we take is seen by the Lord. In a world full of coldness and sadness, God can give you warmth, peace, and happiness. You will find that the "coldness" isn't so bad because it reminds you to appreciate the warmth of the Lord.

Key Verse

"Many of the Samaritans from that town believed in him because of the woman's testimony, 'He told me everything I ever did.'"

John 4:39 NIV

Bible Study

Read John 4:1-42.

Who wrote the book of John?

Who was the author's original audience?

When was the book written?

Look at verses 1-6.

What did the Pharisees hear about Jesus? What do you learn from John 3:22 and 3:26 that gives you more insight?

Where did Jesus go after leaving Judea? What place did Jesus have to travel through to get to there?

What did Jesus do when he got to Sychar? Gain more insight

on Sychar by reading the cross-references.

Genesis 33:18-19; 48:21-22
Joshua 24:32

What time of day did Jesus arrive to Sychar?

Look at verses 7-26.

Who came to draw water from Jacob's well? What did Jesus ask her?

What did the Samaritan woman say to Jesus? Gain more insight about her response by reading the cross-references. Was it common for Samaritans and Jews to converse?

Matthew 10:5-8

Luke 9:51-55

What did Jesus say to her in verse 10? Gain more insight about this verse by looking at the cross-references.

Isaiah 44:3

Jeremiah 2:13

Zechariah 14:8

John 7:37, 38

Revelation 21:6; 22:1, 17

What did the woman say to Jesus next? Did she "get" what Jesus was saying at the time?

How did Jesus respond in verse 13? Learn more from the cross-references listed.

John 6:35

John 7:38

Matthew 25:46

What did the woman say in verse 15? Did she "get" Jesus' message?

How does the conversation continue in verses 16-18? What does Jesus share with her?

What did the woman think of Jesus in verse 19? Why?

What did Jesus reveal to the woman about worshiping in verse 21? What else can you learn from the cross-references?

Matthew 21:11

Deuteronomy 11:29

Josiah 8:33

Luke 9:53

John 5:28, 16:2

Malachi 1:11

1 Titus 2:8

2 Kings 17:28-41

Isaiah 2:3

Romans 3:1-2; 9:45

John 5:25; 16:32

Philippians 3:3

Matthew 1:16

Look at verses 27-38.

When the disciples returned, how did they react in verse 27?

What did the woman do in verses 28-29? What did she leave behind? What does this tell you about her feelings in that moment?

Who came out of town to see Jesus in verse 30? How did they know he was there?

How did Jesus respond when the disciples encouraged him to eat? Why did Jesus respond this way in verse 32?

In verse 33, did the disciples "get" what Jesus was saying?

How did Jesus explain his "food" in verse 34? What else is Jesus teaching the people? Learn more by reviewing the cross-references in the list.

Matthew 9:37, 25:46; 26:39
John 6:38; 19:30
Luke 10:2
Romans 1:13
Job 31:8

Who are the laborers? What is the harvest? What is Jesus teaching about sharing your faith?

Look at verses 39-42.

Why did the Samaritans from the town believe in Jesus?

Why did they want Jesus to stay? How long did he stay?

Why is testifying about your encounter with Jesus important for daily living? When you testify, how should you feel about it? How did the Samaritan woman at Jacob's well, feel about it?

If you haven't already done so, take time to read Biblical commentaries or other cross-references, as needed, to help you consolidate what you learned.

Reflect on Key Question

How can you share your encounter with God and reflect your belief in Christ by your testimony?

Closing Prayer

Lord Jesus, thank you for manifesting who you are in my life! Yes, I have been through many ups and downs. However, you know about all of them! You know my past, my current state, and my future. You hold my life in your hands. You are my Savior! The woman at the well learned about drinking from water and never having to thirst again. Whoooo! I will never want or need anything because I have you! You were not just a prophet; you were the Messiah in the flesh! God himself, as flesh.

The same thing you did for the Samaritans in the town in those days is the same thing you can do for me and my circle of loved ones right now. I will testify about who you are! Watch over me this week as I walk in your goodness. I have comfort in knowing my sins are forgiven, and I won't turn back. I am saved, and my light will shine! In Jesus name, amen!

Week 11: If You Go, I'll Go.

Key Question

How do I surround myself with people who reflect Godly wisdom? How can God use me to lead others?

Opening Prayer

Lord, you are so intentional. Your word speaks, and my heart cannot help but listen to the wisdom in store for me. I ask that the Holy Spirit dwells in my heart. May it flow through me and let nothing distract me from your leadership as I prepare for the study of your word. You will clarify meaning for my life and those I consider to be wise counsel. You will also show me how to lead under your directives and no one else's. Thank you for being my guide all the days of my life. In Jesus' name, Amen!

Devotion

As a person who has worked with children at all levels, I find that all children have capacity to lead. For example, my children do not share the same personalities; however, they both have influence that draws people to them.

If there is one thing about my daughter, she is certainly a leader. When it comes to following a crowd, do not expect her to follow suit. She has always been a little woman ahead of her years. One day, she came to me and said, "Mommy, we are going to McDonald's today." I told tell her, "Who told you that? A Mickey D's trip is not on the schedule." Lo and behold! Guess who ends up at McDonald's that same day. My daughter. How did it happen? Is she a prophetess? We shall see! I will say this: My daughter is charming and great at leading people subtly. She charmed her father into taking her to Mickey D's. It works for her! When it comes to some people, however, she is a straight shooter. Please do not bring your feelings to the table. She will just tell you the truth in raw form. Do we need this bold personality in the world? Of course!

My son, on the other hand, is more diplomatic. He is flexible with adapting to people's personalities, unlike his sister. He is the type to ask reflective questions to capture a better understanding of those he influences. I will say, however, he is selective in his approach and differentiates. In other words, my son reads people and the situation. He has developed a good sense of discernment and is great at navigating different personalities in a productive way. Do we need this type of personality in the world! Of course!

No matter how uniquely different my children are, they were both designed by God to lead. All Christians in the body of Christ were born for a purpose, to lead people to Christ. Whatever one's role may be or whoever one's "fish" may be is determined by the Lord. My daughter's "straight-to-the-point" and "listen to this directive" personality will cater to people who relate to her and desire strong leadership. Marco's diplomatic and supportive personality will cater to people who desire feeling valued and respected. However, we should never be biased or question who God appoints to lead. He qualifies who leads by his standards, not the standards of people.

Often, our selfish ambitions, prejudices, and politics hinder the work of the Lord. We judge who God appoints. I will tell you that if God called you to a position or to act for a purpose, do not let people's opinion of you get in the way. You serve a greater purpose, and you were not born to please man. You were created to walk under the authority of Yahweh, the supreme God. Therefore, I rely on God to provide wisdom for my family concerning how we lead for his kingdom. Do you?

Key Verses

"Barak said to her, 'If you go with me, I will go; but if you don't go with me, I won't go.' 'Certainly, I will go with you,' said Deborah..."

Judges 4:8-9

Bible Study

Read Judges 4:1-24.

Who wrote the book of Judges?

Who is the author's original audience?

When was the book written?

Read verses 1-5.

How does verse 4 begin? What can be said about the history of the Israelites?

What did the Lord allow due to the Israelites' sins?

Who oppressed the Israelites in verse 3? For how long?

Why did the Israelites cry out to the Lord?

Who is Deborah? Why is she significant?

Who did she send for in verse 6? Why? Review Psalms 83:9 for more insight.

What is important about Barak's statement in verse 7? How does he view Deborah?

How did Deborah respond in verse 9? Why is her statement interesting?

Summarize what happens in verses 10-13. Pay close attention to verse 11. Who pitches a tent? Where?

What did Deborah say in verse 14? What did Barak do?

Read verses 16-24.

What happens in verse 16?

Where did Sisera go? To who's tent did he seek help? Why?

Recall verse 11. What happens in verses 18-21? Was Deborah right about what would happen?

Summarize what happens in verses 21-24.

What does this story tell you about God's character when his people cry out to him? Does he keep his promises?

Reflect on Key Question

How do I surround myself with people who reflect Godly wisdom? How can God use me to lead others?

Closing Prayer

Lord, I have been blessed with another Bible story! You never cease to amaze me! You are remarkable considering your orchestration of victory for your people. Your wise counsel and positioning of the right people in the right places at the right time is beyond all my understanding. I praise you for victory in advance. I can cry out to you, and you will respond! Help me lead in your kingdom. I will go, if you, Lord, go with me! In Jesus' name, Amen!

Week 12: I Can't Throw

Key Question

How does Jesus view people who judge others unfairly? How does Jesus see me if I am the one being mistreated and judged unfairly?

Opening Prayer

Lord Jesus, if I have ever treated someone unfairly or gossiped about others' sins knowingly or unknowingly, I ask you for forgiveness. Unveil to me how I should treat people and reflect your humility. If I am ever the object of such treatment, Lord, be there to shield me from others' stones. Soften their hearts to see that we are all flawed, but we can all be made new. Continue to refine us by your word that sanctifies us. In Jesus name, amen!

Devotion

When my brother and I were younger, we played sports every season. Specifically, we played baseball and softball. At the end of February or at the beginning of March, registration for Dixie Youth Baseball would become available. We were both pretty good players. However, I really admired my brother.

One year, when my brother was 12, his team made it all the way to the World Series in South Carolina. He was an excellent player! He played short-stop, and he pitched. My mom used to call him "Shot Gun" because she said, "He could shoot em' before they run!" You know! Like the old-school song! My mother had a sense of humor like no other.

As appropriate as it is to throw a baseball in a ball game, it is not Godly to condemn people by our own measure and throw stones. Whether these stones are real or metaphoric, it isn't okay. The saying, "Sticks and stones may break my bones, but words will never hurt me," isn't true. The truth is that sticks, stones, and words all hurt.

Can you imagine being placed in front of an angry crowd of people and waiting to be stoned to death due to your sin? Think about the thoughts that would ravage your head as you scan people before they stone you. You would likely know some people in the crowd who committed the same sins as you, but they weren't caught. Their dirty laundry wasn't aired and put on display. Thank God Jesus responds to situations such as these.

Key Verse

"Let anyone of you who is without sin be the first to throw a stone at her."

John 8:7 NIV

Bible Study

Read John 8:1-11.

Who wrote the book of John?

Who was the author's original audience?

When was the book written?

Look at verses 1-11.

Where did Jesus go in verse 1? See Matthew 21:1 for more insight.

What did Jesus do in verse 2? Who was gathered around? See Matthew 26:55 for more insight.

What did the Pharisees and teachers of the law do in verse

3? What was their justification for doing this? Review the cross-references to learn more.

Leviticus 20:10

Deuteronomy 22:22

What did the Pharisees and teachers of the law say to Jesus in verses 4 and 5? Now, read verse 6 carefully. What was their agenda?

What did Jesus do in verse 6? What did the Pharisees and teachers of the law continue to do in verse 7? Imagine this scene! Look at the cross-references to learn more.

Matthew 22:15, 18

Matthew 12:10

What did Jesus say in verse 7? What did he continue to do in verse 8? Look at these cross-references for more insight.

Deuteronomy 17:7

Romans 2:1, 22

What happens in verse 9? Why? Who was left?

What did Jesus tell the woman who was left with him? (Didn't God just checkmate some demons?! Ah!)

What did the woman say to Jesus in verse 11? What did Jesus say to her?

What did this reading teach you about judging others? How does it provide comfort if you are the one being judged? Isn't God good?!

Reflect on Key Question

How does Jesus see people who judge others unfairly? How does Jesus see me if I am the one being mistreated and judged unfairly?

Closing Prayer

Lord Jesus, thank you for humbling me and reminding me that I should not judge others by my own measure. Additionally, I am grateful for your protection when people mistreat me or judge me unfairly. We all fall short of the glory of God. The only man without sin to dwell on earth was you. I praise you, and I have joy because I serve a God like you! In Jesus' name, Amen!

Week 13: Time for Intercession

Key Question

How can I serve you with prayer, fasting, and obedience, instead of fear, to intercede for others?

Opening Prayer

Lord, you are three in one: God the Father, God the Son, and God the Holy Spirit. You create a space for unlikely people to do courageous things in your name. You give people support through loved ones to be brave, overcoming fear planted by Satan. As I approach this Bible study, open my heart. Align my will with your will. May I be emboldened to do the will of my Father in heaven. In Jesus' name, Amen!

Devotion

Well, we have entered the last week of winter! Some of us have been itching for the season to change. Goodbye, cold weather! Hello, warmer and brighter days!

As we close out one season and begin a new one, people we know may not be prepared for the season ahead due to factors besides weather. Maybe you or someone you know received some unfavorable news or need encouragement due to uncertainties about the future. What should our response be to these uncertainties? Think about what you have done in the past based on your perspective versus God's perspective. How did things turn out for you when you operated with your own knowledge? Were the results desirable?

As you prepare to read about Esther and her predicament, ask yourself this: "Have I ever felt pressure to move on behalf of others, but there was a lot at stake for me?" Reflect on your first reaction. Would you save yourself and take the easy way out? On the other hand, could God be doing something much greater because he has a bird's eye view as the sovereign one? When we see from our eyes, we miss the greater picture. God's perspective is always best. Fast, pray, and believe.

Key Verse

"For if you remain silent at this time, relief and deliverance for the Jews will arise from another place, but you and your father's family will perish. And who knows but that you have come to your royal position for such a time as this?"

Esther 4:14 NIV

Bible Study

Read Esther 4:1-17.

Read Esther 5: 1-14.
Read Esther 6:1-14.
Read Esther 7:1-9.

Who wrote the book of Esther?

Who was the author's original audience?

When was the book written?

Read Esther 4: 1-17.

How does the reading begin? How is Mordecai feeling in verse 1? Read the cross-references to gain insight and context.

Esther 2: 19-23.
Esther 3:3-6.

What happened in verses 4-6?

Who met Mordecai at the king's gate in verse 6? What does Mordecai share in verses 7-8?

What did Hathak do in verse 9? What did Esther say in verses 10-11?

How did Mordecai respond to Esther's message in verses 12-14? What did this mean for Esther?

What was the message Esther sent back to Mordecai in versus 15-16?

Did Mordecai listen to Esther? Why? What does Esther and Mordecai know about the power of fasting?

Read Esther 5: 1-14.

What happens in verses 1 and 2? Review the cross-references for more enlightenment.

Esther 4:11, 16; 6:4; 8:4
Ezekiel 16: 13
Proverbs 21:1

Was Esther feeling pressure before approaching the king?
Do you believe she felt relief in verse 2?
What did the king say in verse 3?

Summarize what happens in verses 4-7. What does this tell you about King Xerxes' feelings toward Esther?

What happens in verses 9-14? What was Haman's plot?

Read Esther 6:1-12.

What happened in verses 1-3? What did King Xerxes learn about Mordecai?

Who appears in verse 4? Why was he there?

Summarize what happens in verses 6-12. How is Haman feeling? What did Haman's wife say?

Read Esther 7:1-9.

Summarize the conversation between Esther and King Xerxes in verses 1-7. How did the atmosphere at the banquet shift? What did Haman ask of Esther?

What happened in verses 8-9? What happened to Haman?

Read Esther 8:1-8.

What does this tell you about the all-powerful God you serve?

Reflect on Key Question

How can I serve you with prayer, fasting, and obedience, instead of fear, to intercede for others?

Closing Prayer

Lord, Esther navigated a very difficult situation and acted on behalf of her people. You positioned her, allowing her to become queen and intercede. You guided her cousin Mordecai to provide Esther wisdom. You put an unlikely leader in place to thwart the enemy's plan of slaughtering your beloved children. Oh, how you turn things around!

Help me step up to the plate to intercede for others through fasting, prayer, and action. I know I will be successful if you are with me. If I perish in your name, I perish. I live for a greater purpose than a physical death. All humans will have that end. My greater purpose is spiritual life in you! This life is eternal. In Jesus' name, Amen!

See You Next Season

Dear Spiritual Sister,

You made it through 13-weeks of devotions and in-depth Bible studies! I pray you have been empowered with the word of God in this winter season. You have applied this knowledge as a living sacrifice for the Lord. Together, we can walk boldly in the fullness of God through fasting, praying, and obedience! Once you have tasted God's goodness, there is no turning back. While seasons may change in our lives, remember God remains the same. He is an anchor for your soul. An ever-present help in time of need! An ever-present help indeed! Glory to God. Sometimes, I shout and dance because of God's goodness.

Remember, God sees you. Every heartache, every celebration, every sin, and every righteous act. He can tell you everything you ever did from a baby being developed in your mother's womb until now. You live under the authority of a gracious, good Father. You are his daughter, and he wants you to seek him in all seasons of your life, not just the ups and not just the downs. All seasons! As the weather starts to warm up over the next few weeks, observe how God changes the weather. The snow melts and animals no longer hibernate. Spring draws near and flowers begin to bloom. Isn't God just amazing? Think of all the things his hands have made, including you.

Leave whatever burdens you carry at the altar. Go to God in prayer and ask for forgiveness of sins known and unknown. God renews your spirit, and you are saved through faith because of your belief in Jesus. He came down as flesh, died for our sins, and rose again! Evidence of your faith is in your daily behavior and walk with God. Do not fear. Just believe.

If you needed another spiritual sister, you have one in me. We could always use more! Let's stay connected. Until next season…

Your Spiritual Sister,

Valeece

Acknowledgement

This book would not exist if it were not for support in my corner. I acknowledge two of my favorite people who have poured into me during the most difficult times of my life. They have been steady and supportive, continuously sharpening me to align my resources and talents with God's word. For this, I am grateful.

Firstly, I acknowledge my husband Jarome of 11 years. He is the one I love most besides Jesus of course. He has supported me in more ways than one throughout our marriage. He has taken precious time to review drafts of my manuscripts and listen to all God has planted in my heart.

When I told my husband I was completing this book, he never wavered on support even though he may have thought I was a bit crazy! I had several nights of working late, and I would run on fumes during the day. This was all due to the stirring in my spirit behind the great work God was doing in me. Constant, awesome thoughts would just flow from my mouth at random times, and my husband simply listened. When I told him about the yearning I had for God, he did not understand all my fragmented thoughts, but because of the evidence of things happening in our lives at the time, he credited it to God. Many men cannot understand the ways of such a persistent wife on matters about the Lord, but Jarome does. I thank God for him.

Next, I acknowledge Whitney Marie, my best friend and "spiritual sister twin" since the fourth grade. Not only is she my sister from the same mister (God Almighty), but she has always been the encouragement I needed at just the right time. Her words bless my soul daily. Yes, we talk daily! She has a heart of gold that chases God like I have never seen. Because Whitney is blessed with a heart seeking after the Lord, I am inspired from her overflow of blessings due to God's work in her. This goodness spills over to me. The study of God's word is contagious! She and I love studying, and we never cease to share testimonies and wisdom with each other. Due to Whitney's gentle pushes, I have finally planned and intentionally published my first book.

For these reasons, I found it only appropriate to acknowledge my husband Jarome and my dear sister, Whitney Marie. Finally, I look forward to authoring several more books. This is just the beginning.

Books In This Series

God in Seasons for Women

This series is for women of faith who marvel at the work of God's hands as the seasons change throughout the year and in life. This 4-book collection will keep you encouraged and inspired to study God's word in a way you never have experienced. Be confident and led by the Holy Spirit to study the Holy Bible intentionally. Whether a woman is new to studying the Bible or a veteran at studying the Bible, she will enjoy 13 weeks of devotions and Bible studies for each season of the year: winter, spring, summer, and fall!

God In The Winter: 13 Devotionals & Bible Studies For Women

God In The Spring: 13 Devotionals & Bible Studies For Women

God In The Summer: 13 Devotionals & Bible Studies For Women

God In The Fall: 13 Devotionals & Bible Studies For Women

Made in the USA
Columbia, SC
17 March 2025

55199005R00046